Mastering Real Estate Investment.

Jack L. Green

Jack L. Green.

INTRODUCTION

In a world driven by dynamic financial landscapes, where opportunities emerge and evolve in the blink of an eye, there stands an age-old pillar of wealth creation that has weathered the storms of time: real estate. And within the vast realm of real estate investment, few strategies offer the promise of enduring prosperity quite like the art and science of intelligent rental property investing. Welcome, dear reader, to a transformational journey guided by the pages of "Mastering Real Estate Investment."

1.   Unlocking the Power of Buy-and-Hold Real Estate Investing

At the heart of this journey lies the power of buy-and-hold real estate investing. The concept isn't just about property; it's about possessing a tangible asset that appreciates over time, generating a steady stream of income while concurrently building equity. With each property, you're not merely buying a structure; you're investing in your financial future, nurturing a resource that grows in value even as it provides for you.

2.   Setting Your Goals and Cultivating the Right Mindset

But financial success isn't built on properties alone; it's also built on the foundation of your goals and mindset. Within the pages of this book, we'll explore how setting clear objectives and adopting the right mindset can shape the trajectory of your investments. Your goals become your roadmap, guiding you through the labyrinth of decisions and strategies. And your mindset becomes the fuel that propels you forward, transforming challenges into opportunities and setbacks into stepping stones.

Imagine a life where your money works for you, where bricks and mortar become a canvas for your financial dreams. This book is your key to unlocking that life – a life that whispers of financial freedom, wealth accumulation, and the realization of your most audacious aspirations. It's a world where properties become not just dwellings, but assets; where the walls around you echo with the sound of growing income streams and the tangible proof of a life well-invested.

"Mastering Real Estate Investment" is not just a compilation of knowledge; it's a roadmap to navigating the intricate landscape of real estate, one that has been paved with years of experience, insight, and triumphs. Whether you're a seasoned investor aiming to diversify your portfolio or a newcomer seeking to harness the potential of rental properties, this book is your trusted guide, your beacon through the fog of uncertainty.

Within these pages, you'll journey through the fundamentals of real estate markets, learning to read their pulse and anticipate their shifts. You'll discover the art of property selection and analysis, understanding how to discern the diamonds from the rough. We'll dive into the nuances of financing your investments, decoding the labyrinthine world of mortgages and interest rates. Armed with this knowledge, you'll be primed to make intelligent investment decisions that resonate with your financial objectives.

But what truly sets this book apart is its commitment to holistic success. We don't just throw you into the ocean of investment and hope you swim; we provide the life vests that ensure you navigate the waves with confidence. From tenant selection and lease agreements to the management of properties and the fine art of maximizing cash flow, our goal is not just to initiate success but to nurture and sustain it.

Scaling your real estate empire is not a mere concept here – it's a reality we'll help you shape. With strategies for expansion, refinancing, and the creation of efficient systems, you'll master the art of growth in a way that bolsters your financial goals. And as you soar, we'll be there to help you navigate the challenges and risks that come your way, from vacancies to legal complexities, ensuring you emerge stronger and more resilient.

At the heart of "Mastering Real Estate Investment" lies the promise of a better future – one where you're not beholden to the whims of traditional employment or the caprices of market volatility. It's a future where you hold the reins, where every property is a step toward creating a legacy of financial independence, not just for yourself but for generations to come.

So, embark on this journey with us. Let the knowledge within these pages be the foundation upon which you build your real estate empire. Let it be the catalyst for a life that transcends boundaries and limitations. Let "Mastering Real Estate Investment" be your guide, your confidant, and your companion on the path to real estate prosperity. Your journey to a brighter financial future begins now.

CHAPTER ONE

Four illustrations of plans:

In a world where financial freedom and wealth creation have become key goals, the realm of real estate investment stands as a promising gateway. Among the myriad paths open to investors, rental property investing offers a unique avenue that combines steady income generation, possible appreciation, and long-term wealth accumulation. Aspiring investors, however, often find themselves navigating a complex landscape with numerous factors to consider. This book, "Mastering Real Estate Investment: A Guide to Rental Property Success," aims to demystify the journey, offering a comprehensive roadmap with four distinct plans to empower readers on their path to success.

Plan 1: Breaking into Homes:

The journey of a rental property investor starts with the crucial step of breaking into the market. While the idea of property acquisition may seem daunting, a well-structured plan can help pave the way for a successful start. This part of the book will delve into the fundamental aspects that an aspiring investor needs to consider when taking their first steps in the world of real estate.

Market Research:

A solid foundation for any real estate endeavor starts with thorough market study. Understanding the local market trends, demand, and supply dynamics, as well as economic factors that influence the rental property market, is important. This section will guide readers through the process of gathering relevant data, analyzing market trends, and finding neighborhoods with growth potential.

Property Selection:

Choosing the right property is akin to choosing a cornerstone for your investment journey. From single-family homes to multi-unit complexes, there are a myriad of choices available. This part of the plan will equip readers with criteria to evaluate properties, such as location, property condition, potential for value appreciation, and alignment with investment goals.

Financing Strategies:

The financial part of real estate investment can be both complex and pivotal. Many investors face challenges related to getting financing for their ventures. In this section, readers will explore various financing choices, including traditional mortgages, private lenders, partnerships, and creative financing methods. Understanding the pros and cons of each method will empower investors to make informed choices that align with their financial capabilities and risk tolerance.

Building a Network:

Real estate investment is rarely a solitary activity. Building a network of professionals, from real estate agents and property managers to contractors and legal advisors, can greatly enhance an investor's chances of success. This part of the plan will emphasize the importance of cultivating relationships within the industry, giving insights into how to identify reliable partners and collaborators.

Overcoming Challenges:

Breaking into the rental property market is not without its difficulties. Unexpected hurdles and obstacles are natural. Readers will benefit from learning about common challenges met by novice investors and strategies to overcome them. Whether it's dealing with property maintenance, tenant issues, or economic downturns, knowing how to navigate these hurdles is crucial for sustained success.

Conclusion:

Embarking on the road of rental property investing requires a thoughtful approach and a well-defined plan. The first plan described in this book, "Breaking into Homes," lays the groundwork for aspiring investors to navigate the complexities of the real estate market. By conducting thorough market research, selecting properties strategically, exploring financing options, building a reliable network, and preparing for challenges, investors can position themselves for success in their goal of rental property investment. As we move forward, the subsequent plans will delve into more advanced strategies, guiding readers toward greater financial milestones and eventually, mastery of the art of rental property investing.

Plan 2: Investing in Single-Family Homes to Build Wealth:

Rental property investment holds the potential to unlock a world of financial possibilities, and one route that has consistently proven its worth is investing in single-family homes. While multifamily units and commercial properties also offer attractive possibilities, single-family homes have their own set of advantages that make them an appealing choice for investors looking to build wealth steadily over time.

Advantages of Single-Family Homes:

Investing in single-family homes offers several distinct advantages that contribute to their popularity among investors. One key advantage is the broader pool of potential tenants. Single-family homes attract a diverse range of renters, from young professionals and families to empty nesters and retirees. This broad appeal enhances the likelihood of maintaining consistent occupancy rates, reducing the risk of income gaps.

1. Location, Location, Location:

The age-old adage in real estate, "location, location, location," holds true for single-family homes as well. Choosing the right location significantly impacts the potential for property appreciation and tenant demand. Investors should target areas with strong job markets, good schools, access to amenities, and overall positive growth indicators. This section of the plan will delve into the importance of location selection and provide tips for identifying areas with strong investment potential.

2. Property Management Considerations:

Owning and managing single-family homes involves unique considerations compared to other property types. Investors must navigate property maintenance, tenant relations, and logistical challenges. This part of the plan will discuss strategies for effective property management, from maintaining curb appeal to addressing tenant needs promptly. It will also explore the benefits of outsourcing property management tasks versus managing properties independently.

3. Diversification and Risk Mitigation:

Investors often hear the advice to diversify their portfolios, and single-family homes offer a natural means of achieving diversification within the real estate realm. Spreading investments across multiple single-family properties in different locations can help mitigate risk by reducing the impact of localized market fluctuations. This segment of the plan will delve into diversification strategies, emphasizing the importance of a balanced and well-considered approach.

4. Financial Benefits of Single-Family Homes:

The financial benefits of investing in single-family homes are multifaceted. This section will explore the potential for generating passive income through rental payments, building equity through mortgage payments, and benefiting from potential property appreciation. The plan will also touch upon the tax advantages associated with rental property ownership, including deductions for property-related expenses and depreciation.

5. Scaling the Single-Family Home Portfolio:

As investors gain experience and confidence, scaling their portfolios becomes a logical progression. This final portion of the plan will offer insights into strategies for scaling a single-family home portfolio. It will address considerations such as financing options for acquiring additional properties, managing an expanding portfolio, and adjusting investment strategies based on market dynamics and personal goals.

Conclusion:

Investing in single-family homes provides a dynamic pathway to building wealth through rental property investment. This plan has shed light on the advantages that single-family homes offer, from their broad tenant appeal to the potential for property appreciation. By selecting prime locations, mastering property management, diversifying portfolios, and understanding the financial benefits, investors can harness the power of single-family homes to achieve their wealth-building goals. As we journey through the subsequent plans, we will uncover further strategies that continue to elevate the art of rental property investing, ultimately guiding readers towards mastering the intricacies of the real estate market.

Plan 3: Using Rental Properties to Earn $1,000,000:

Unlocking the potential of rental properties as a means to achieve significant financial milestones is a compelling objective for many investors. Plan 3 delves into a strategic approach that aims to leverage rental properties to earn a substantial sum of $1,000,000. This plan focuses on combining effective property selection, cash flow optimization, property appreciation, and scaling strategies to reach this ambitious financial goal.

1. Strategic Property Selection:

The cornerstone of this plan is selecting properties that align with the objective of earning $1,000,000. Properties with strong potential for value appreciation and steady rental income are paramount. This section will discuss strategies for identifying properties in emerging neighborhoods, considering property types that attract high-demand tenants, and conducting thorough due diligence to ensure each property's investment potential.

2. Cash Flow Optimization:

Generating consistent cash flow is a key component of this plan. Properly setting rental rates, minimizing vacancies, and managing expenses are critical factors in achieving positive cash flow. This segment will delve into techniques for optimizing rental income, ensuring that monthly rental revenue exceeds operational costs and mortgage payments, contributing to the overall objective of accumulating $1,000,000.

3. Property Appreciation Strategies:

Property appreciation adds another layer of potential wealth generation to the plan. This section will explore ways to enhance property value through strategic renovations, upgrades, and curb appeal improvements. Additionally, it will touch upon factors like market trends, economic indicators, and the role of neighborhood development in influencing property appreciation.

4. Leveraging Tax Benefits:

Utilizing tax benefits inherent to rental property ownership can significantly contribute to the accumulation of wealth. This part of the plan will provide an overview of tax deductions available to rental property owners, such as deductions for mortgage interest, property management expenses, and depreciation. By effectively leveraging these deductions, investors can maximize their after-tax cash flow and accelerate their progress toward the $1,000,000 goal.

5. Scaling the Portfolio:

To reach the $1,000,000 milestone, scaling the rental property portfolio becomes essential. This section will discuss strategies for expanding the portfolio over time, such as refinancing existing properties to fund new acquisitions, leveraging equity, and reinvesting rental income. It will also cover the importance of managing the portfolio's growth to ensure sustainable and efficient operations.

6. Monitoring and Adjusting the Plan:

Adaptability is crucial in any investment journey. This part of the plan will emphasize the importance of monitoring progress regularly and making necessary adjustments. It will guide readers on how to assess the performance of their properties, identify areas for improvement, and pivot their strategies based on evolving market conditions or personal goals.

Conclusion:

Using rental properties as a vehicle to earn $1,000,000 requires a strategic approach that combines smart property selection, effective cash flow management, property appreciation tactics, tax optimization, and deliberate scaling strategies. Plan 3 provides readers with a comprehensive roadmap to navigate the complexities of achieving this financial milestone. By aligning each step of the plan with the overarching goal and staying attuned to market dynamics, investors can harness the power of rental properties to transform their financial aspirations into reality. As we continue to explore the subsequent plans, readers will uncover further strategies and insights that continue to elevate their prowess in the realm of rental property investing.

Plan 4: Using the BRRR Approach to Earn $100,000 Each Year

Plan 4 introduces a powerful strategy that holds the potential to generate consistent income: the BRRR approach (Buy, Rehab, Rent, Refinance). This strategy involves a series of well-defined steps that, when executed effectively, can lead to substantial returns on investment. By following the BRRR approach meticulously, investors can aim to achieve an impressive annual income of $100,0000.

1. **Understanding the BRRR Approach:**

The BRRR approach is a systematic method that involves purchasing a property, rehabilitating it to increase its value, placing tenants in the property to generate rental income, and then refinancing to recover a substantial portion of the initial investment. This recycled capital can then be reinvested in additional properties, effectively compounding returns over time.

2. **Buying Right:**

The foundation of the BRRR approach lies in acquiring properties at the right price. This involves thorough market research to identify undervalued properties with potential for appreciation after renovations. This section of the plan will delve into strategies for finding distressed properties, conducting due diligence, and negotiating favorable purchase terms.

3. Rehabilitation for Value Enhancement:

The "R" in BRRR stands for "Rehab," and it's a critical phase where investors breathe new life into the property. This segment will discuss rehab strategies that yield the highest return on investment, from cosmetic upgrades like fresh paint and new flooring to more substantial improvements such as kitchen and bathroom renovations. Proper budgeting, project management, and attention to detail are key factors in maximizing the property's value during this phase.

4. Generating Rental Income:

Once the property is renovated, the focus shifts to generating rental income. This part of the plan will cover tenant selection, property management considerations, and strategies for setting competitive rental rates. Maintaining a positive landlord-tenant relationship is vital for a successful rental property venture.

5. Refinancing for Capital Recovery:

The "Refinance" step is where the BRRR approach truly shines. After increasing the property's value through rehabilitation and renting it out, investors can refinance the property based on its new appraised value. This can potentially allow them to recoup a significant portion of their initial investment. The plan will explore refinancing strategies, the role of lenders, and how this recovered capital can be reinvested in additional properties.

6. Scaling the BRRR Strategy:

The BRRR approach's power lies in its scalability. This segment of the plan will discuss how investors can replicate the BRRR process to acquire multiple properties over time. By using the recycled capital from refinancing one property to fund the purchase and rehabilitation of another, investors can compound their portfolio and ultimately increase their income potential.

7. **Mitigating Risks and Challenges:**

While the BRRR approach offers lucrative potential, it's not without risks. This part of the plan will address potential challenges such as project delays, budget overruns, and market fluctuations. Strategies for mitigating these risks, conducting thorough risk assessments, and having contingency plans will be discussed.

Conclusion:

The BRRR approach is a dynamic strategy that empowers investors to generate significant income through strategic property acquisition, value enhancement, rental income, and capital recovery. By mastering the art of buying right, rehabilitating effectively, generating rental income, and refinancing strategically, investors can aim to earn $100,000 annually and beyond. As we delve deeper into the intricacies of this approach and continue to explore advanced investment strategies, readers will gain the tools and knowledge to excel in the world of rental property investing. Through the BRRR approach, investors have the potential to not only achieve their financial goals but also create a sustainable path to long-term wealth accumulation.

CHAPTER TWO

Understanding Real Estate Markets: Navigating the Path to Profit

In the captivating world of real estate investment, where fortunes can be made and dreams realized, there exists a crucial cornerstone that separates the novice from the adept: understanding real estate markets. The concept goes beyond mere location; it encompasses a comprehensive grasp of market trends, economic indicators, and growth opportunities. In this chapter, we embark on a journey of exploration, delving into the intricacies of understanding real estate markets to navigate the path to profit.

- Researching Market Trends: Illuminating the Landscape

To master the art of real estate investment, one must first become a detective of market trends. The ever-shifting currents of supply and demand, coupled with socioeconomic changes, shape the real estate landscape. Thus, the astute investor learns to read between the lines, identify patterns, and anticipate shifts. This involves diligent research, an unquenchable thirst for information, and an ability to interpret data that often hides in plain sight.

Peering into the dynamics of a market requires a multifaceted approach. It's not merely about observing the number of "For Sale" signs lining a neighborhood; it's about understanding the stories those signs tell. Are they indicative of a market oversaturation or a sudden surge in demand? Scrutinizing recent sales data, rental rates, and occupancy rates helps paint a vivid picture of a market's health.

Moreover, real estate trends don't exist in a vacuum; they're closely intertwined with broader societal shifts. Consider urbanization, for instance. As more people flock to cities, the demand for housing increases, potentially leading to higher property values and rental rates. Conversely, in certain regions, the rise of remote work might trigger a demand for suburban or rural properties that offer a reprieve from congested urban centers.

Beyond the quantitative, it's crucial to uncover qualitative factors. Demographic trends, employment opportunities, infrastructure development, and the overall vibe of a neighborhood play pivotal roles in market attractiveness. The art is in distilling these factors into a coherent narrative that guides your investment decisions. By researching market trends, you're not just passively observing; you're engaging with the dynamic symphony of data and transforming it into a tune that resonates with your investment strategy.

- Evaluating Economic Indicators: The Pulse of Prosperity

Just as a physician listens to a patient's heartbeat to gauge their health, a real estate investor listens to economic indicators to gauge the financial pulse of a market. These indicators are the vital signs of a region's economic well-being, offering insights into its potential for growth and stability. From employment rates and wage growth to inflation rates and consumer confidence, economic indicators paint a holistic picture of a market's viability.

For instance, a booming job market signifies increased demand for housing, potentially driving up property prices and rental rates. Conversely, stagnation or a sudden downturn in employment might trigger a decline in demand, affecting your investment's profitability. By evaluating economic indicators, you're not merely reacting to market shifts; you're proactively positioning yourself to ride the waves of economic prosperity.

Wage growth, another key indicator, is a testament to the overall health of an economy. A region experiencing steady wage growth is likely to attract a stable and growing population, creating a robust demand for housing. Moreover, it signals that residents have more disposable income, potentially leading to increased property values and rental rates. This symbiotic relationship between wage growth and real estate performance is a critical aspect of understanding market dynamics.

Consumer confidence, often measured through surveys and indices, reflects the sentiment of the population towards the economy's future. High consumer confidence indicates optimism, encouraging spending and investment. In the realm of real estate, confident consumers are more likely to make significant financial commitments, such as purchasing a home or investing in rental properties. Therefore, tracking shifts in consumer confidence can provide valuable insights into the trajectory of real estate markets.

- Identifying Growth Opportunities: Where Potential Meets Possibility

Amid the intricate tapestry of real estate markets, growth opportunities lie like hidden gems waiting to be unearthed. Identifying these opportunities requires a blend of foresight, market knowledge, and a willingness to venture beyond the obvious. A market might appear stagnant on the surface, but underneath, a series of revitalization projects might be brewing, poised to breathe new life into the neighborhood.

Spotting growth opportunities involves thinking both macro and micro. On a macro level, it's about aligning your investments with regions that are experiencing population growth, economic development, and a surge in infrastructure projects. For instance, a city undergoing significant urban renewal might present lucrative opportunities for real estate investors, as neighborhoods are revitalized, attracting new residents and businesses.

On a micro level, it's about identifying neighborhoods that are on the cusp of transformation – perhaps a neglected district that's slowly undergoing gentrification or an area adjacent to a burgeoning commercial hub. These micro-level growth opportunities often require a keen eye and a willingness to invest before others catch wind of the potential. It's about embracing calculated risks and being the visionary who sees the future value in properties that others might overlook.

Moreover, the concept extends beyond physical development. It's about understanding trends like the rise of remote work, which might render previously undesirable locations suddenly attractive due to their proximity to natural beauty or recreational facilities. It's about being forward-thinking, envisioning how market dynamics might evolve and positioning yourself accordingly.

In conclusion, understanding real estate markets isn't just about studying graphs and numbers; it's about becoming attuned to the heartbeat of communities, deciphering economic rhythms, and discerning the potential that lies beneath the surface. By researching market trends, evaluating economic indicators, and identifying growth opportunities, you're not just navigating the path to profit – you're becoming a master of real estate investment. Armed with this knowledge, you'll transform the uncertainty of the market into a canvas upon which you'll paint your real estate success story.

CHAPTER THREE

Property Selection and Analysis: Crafting the Foundation of Success

In the intricate tapestry of real estate investment, perhaps no stage is as pivotal as property selection and analysis. This phase represents the canvas upon which your financial future is painted – a canvas that demands meticulous attention, thorough research, and a keen eye for detail. In this chapter, we embark on a journey to unravel the nuances of property selection and analysis, understanding how to discern diamonds from the rough and craft a foundation of success.

• Criteria for Selecting Rental Properties: A Blueprint for Prosperity

To navigate the realm of real estate investment with finesse, one must possess a discerning eye for property selection. The blueprint for prosperity isn't a one-size-fits-all; it's a tapestry woven with specific criteria that align with your investment goals. Each criterion is a thread that contributes to the fabric of your success, and your ability to weave them harmoniously determines the potential of your investment.

Location stands as the cornerstone of property selection. The age-old adage "location, location, location" reverberates through time for a reason. A property's location influences its desirability, rental potential, and potential appreciation. Proximity to essential amenities, educational institutions, public transport, and recreational facilities can elevate a property's appeal, drawing in tenants and ensuring long-term profitability.

Furthermore, the neighborhood's socio-economic environment plays a pivotal role. Researching crime rates, school quality, job opportunities, and community vibes provides invaluable insights. A thriving neighborhood with a strong community fabric tends to attract stable tenants and foster positive growth over time.

Physical condition is another crucial criterion. A property in disrepair might offer a lower upfront cost, but the subsequent costs of repairs and maintenance can erode your profits. On the other hand, properties in good condition might command a higher purchase price, but they often come with lower maintenance costs, better tenant retention, and improved cash flow.

Financial feasibility is the linchpin that holds your investment strategy together. Evaluating the potential rental income, factoring in operating expenses, and calculating potential returns determine whether a property aligns with your financial goals. Understanding metrics like cash flow, cap rates, and return on investment helps you make informed decisions, ensuring that your investment doesn't merely generate income, but does so sustainably.

- **Conducting Comparative Market Analysis: The Art of Informed Decision-Making**

In the symphony of property selection and analysis, conducting a comparative market analysis (CMA) emerges as a powerful instrument. Just as a conductor blends different musical elements to create harmonious melodies, a real estate investor blends data points to create informed decisions. A CMA involves evaluating comparable properties in the market to determine a property's fair market value, guiding you toward making offers that align with the property's true worth.

Comparable properties, often referred to as "comps," serve as benchmarks. These properties are similar in terms of size, location, condition, and features, providing a reference point for assessing your chosen property. Analyzing comps involves examining their recent sales prices, rental income, and overall performance in the market. This comparison allows you to gauge whether the property you're considering is priced fairly or potentially overvalued.

Market trends influence a property's value, and CMAs help you keep your finger on the pulse. If property values in a certain neighborhood are on the rise due to increased demand, your CMA can help you identify this trend and capitalize on it. Similarly, if property values in a certain area have stagnated or declined, your CMA can alert you to potential pitfalls.

Furthermore, a well-constructed CMA serves as a negotiating tool. Armed with data that supports your assessment of a property's value, you're better equipped to negotiate with sellers, ensuring you don't overpay.

Additionally, if your CMA indicates that a property is undervalued, you might have the opportunity to secure a deal that provides built-in equity from the moment of purchase.

- **Evaluating Potential Cash Flow: The Heartbeat of Investment Returns**

Cash flow is the lifeblood of any real estate investment. It's the heartbeat that sustains your investment journey, providing the financial oxygen needed to cover expenses, generate profits, and fuel future growth. Evaluating potential cash flow isn't just a matter of calculating income minus expenses; it's a delicate dance between projections and realities, between aspirations and pragmatism.

The first step in evaluating cash flow is estimating rental income. This involves assessing comparable rental rates for properties of similar size and location, factoring in market demand and your property's unique attributes. Setting the right rental rate ensures your property remains competitive in attracting tenants while generating a steady stream of income.

Operating expenses form the counterbalance to rental income. These expenses encompass a spectrum, including property management fees, maintenance costs, property taxes, insurance, and potential vacancy expenses. Accurate estimation of these costs is crucial for projecting cash flow accurately. Underestimating expenses can lead to unpleasant surprises, whereas overestimating them might deter you from pursuing a potentially profitable investment.

Positive cash flow isn't the sole consideration. Understanding the concept of "break-even point" is equally crucial. This is the point at which your rental income covers all expenses, ensuring your investment isn't draining your resources. Achieving positive cash flow beyond the break-even point is what transforms a property from merely sustainable to truly lucrative.

In conclusion, the stage of property selection and analysis is akin to crafting the foundation of a skyscraper. The criteria you set for property selection provide the blueprint, the CMA offers the structural integrity, and the evaluation of potential cash flow forms the robust structure that supports your investment. By mastering this phase, you're setting the stage for success, ensuring that your investment endeavors are built on solid ground.

CHAPTER FOUR

Financing Your Investments: Navigating the Path to Prosperity

In the intricate landscape of real estate investment, the bridge between aspirations and achievements is built with the stones of strategic financing. From your first property acquisition to the expansion of your portfolio, the decisions you make about financing can either fortify your foundation or become stumbling blocks on your journey. In this chapter, we embark on a journey to understand the different types of real estate financing, the nuances of mortgage options, and the significance of calculating the debt-to-income ratio.

• Types of Real Estate Financing: Crafting Your Financial Palette

Real estate financing is a realm of diverse possibilities, offering a spectrum of avenues to fuel your investment endeavors. Just as a painter selects colors from a palette, you have an array of financial tools at your disposal to craft your investment masterpiece. By understanding these options, you can tailor your approach to align with your investment strategy and goals.

Traditional Mortgages are the bedrock of real estate financing. They involve borrowing from a lending institution to purchase a property, with interest rates and loan terms determined by your financial health and creditworthiness. These mortgages offer a conventional path to property ownership and are favored by investors seeking stability and predictability.

Creative Financing, on the other hand, presents alternative routes. Seller financing allows you to negotiate directly with the property owner, bypassing traditional lenders. Lease options and subject-to financing offer unique strategies to acquire properties with minimal upfront costs, particularly advantageous in competitive markets or when traditional financing avenues are limited.

Private Money Lenders operate outside traditional financial institutions, providing loans based on their capital. These loans can be more flexible than traditional mortgages, offering quicker approvals and less stringent credit requirements. Hard money loans are short-term loans secured by the property itself, often used for rapid acquisitions or renovations.

Crowdfunding Platforms harness the collective investment power of multiple individuals to fund real estate projects. This approach allows you to pool resources for larger investments, diversifying risk and potentially accessing larger capital pools.

- Mortgage Options and Considerations: Building on Solid Ground

Mortgages form the cornerstone of real estate financing, dictating the terms under which you acquire properties. Understanding the nuances of different mortgage options empowers you to make informed decisions that resonate with your financial objectives and investment strategy.

Fixed-Rate Mortgages offer stability, with consistent interest rates over the life of the loan. This predictability ensures your monthly payments remain constant, providing a sense of financial security. However, initial interest rates might be slightly higher than those of adjustable-rate mortgages.

Adjustable Rate Mortgages (ARMs) start with lower interest rates that can adjust periodically. While this can lead to cost savings initially, the potential for rate adjustments introduces an element of uncertainty. ARMs might be suitable for investors who anticipate selling or refinancing before the rates adjust.

The choice between fixed-rate and adjustable-rate mortgages hinges on your risk tolerance, long-term goals, and market conditions. Engaging with a knowledgeable mortgage professional can guide you toward the most suitable option for your investment endeavors.

- Calculating Debt-to-Income Ratio: Balancing Financial Health

The debt-to-income (DTI) ratio is a critical metric that reflects your financial health and determines your borrowing capacity. This ratio compares your monthly debt payments to your monthly income, providing insights into your ability to manage additional financial commitments.

A lower DTI ratio signifies lower financial risk and higher borrowing capacity. Lenders typically prefer borrowers with a DTI ratio below 43%, but individual circumstances can influence this threshold. Calculating your DTI ratio involves summing your monthly debts, including existing mortgage payments, credit card payments, and other loan obligations, and dividing by your monthly pre-tax income.

Maintaining a healthy DTI ratio is essential for securing favorable mortgage terms and ensuring that your investment endeavors remain financially sustainable. A lower DTI ratio not only enhances your eligibility for loans but also strengthens your overall financial resilience.

In Conclusion: Your Financial Compass

As you navigate the complex terrain of financing your real estate investments, keep in mind that your financial choices shape the trajectory of your journey. By exploring various types of real estate financing, understanding mortgage options, and calculating your debt-to-income ratio, you equip yourself with a robust financial compass that guides your decisions. Just as a navigator charts a course through uncharted waters, you'll chart a path to prosperity, leveraging strategic financing to build your real estate empire brick by brick.

CHAPTER FIVE

Making Smart Investment Decisions: A Blueprint for Success

In the dynamic world of real estate investment, the foundation of success is built upon making smart decisions at every turn. From assessing properties to negotiating purchase agreements and navigating property management, each choice shapes your journey toward prosperity. In this chapter, we embark on a journey to understand the significance of due diligence and property inspection, the art of negotiating purchase agreements, and the crucial role of property management.

- ### Due Diligence and Property Inspection: Unveiling the Reality

Embarking on a real estate investment journey requires more than surface-level assessments; it calls for meticulous due diligence and thorough property inspections. Just as an archaeologist uncovers hidden treasures, your due diligence unveils critical insights that influence your investment decisions.

Conducting due diligence involves digging into a property's history, legal status, and financial health. This process unveils potential red flags and offers a deeper understanding of the property's value proposition. Property inspections go hand in hand, involving professional assessments of a property's structural integrity, systems, and condition.

A comprehensive due diligence process encompasses researching property titles, zoning regulations, and potential liens. This uncovers any encumbrances that could impact your investment. Property inspections, on the other hand, uncover hidden defects and provide insights into the property's maintenance requirements.

• Negotiating Purchase Agreements: The Art of Deal Making

The art of negotiation is integral to real estate investment success. Mastering this skill enables you to secure favorable purchase agreements, optimize your terms, and position yourself for long-term profitability. Negotiation isn't just about price; it involves crafting a deal that aligns with your investment goals.

Before negotiations begin, research the property thoroughly. Understand its market value, recent sales of comparable properties, and its unique attributes that could influence negotiations. This knowledge empowers you to negotiate from a position of strength.

Effective negotiation involves clear communication and a willingness to collaborate. Present your offer confidently, emphasizing the value you bring as an investor. Be prepared to make concessions while safeguarding your bottom line. Understand that negotiations are a give-and-take process that can lead to mutually beneficial outcomes.

• Understanding Property Management: The Key to Sustainable Returns

Property management is the bridge between property ownership and financial returns. Effective property management ensures that your investments remain viable, tenants are satisfied, and your cash flow remains consistent. By understanding the nuances of property management, you can enhance your investment's sustainability.

Effective property management involves tasks such as tenant screening, rent collection, maintenance coordination, and conflict resolution. Whether you opt for self-management or engage a property management company, staying informed about best practices is crucial.

Selecting quality tenants is the cornerstone of successful property management. Screen potential tenants thoroughly, checking credit history, references, and rental history. This minimizes the risk of late payments and property damage.

Maintenance is another pivotal aspect. Regular property maintenance not only ensures tenant satisfaction but also preserves the property's value over time. Timely repairs and proactive upkeep contribute to long-term profitability.

In conclusion, the art of making smart investment decisions lies in the meticulous execution of due diligence, skilled negotiation, and effective property management. By unveiling the reality through due diligence and property inspection, mastering the art of deal making, and understanding the dynamics of property management, you're sculpting the blueprint for sustained success in your real estate endeavors. With each decision made, you're not just building structures; you're building a future defined by financial empowerment and real estate achievement.

CHAPTER SIX

Managing Rental Properties: Nurturing Success through Effective Oversight

In the realm of real estate investment, the art of managing rental properties stands as a keystone to long-term success. As you transition from acquiring properties to generating income, the management phase becomes a symphony of responsibilities that require meticulous attention. This chapter delves into the intricacies of managing rental properties, from finding reliable tenants to crafting effective leases, conducting tenant screenings and background checks, and adeptly handling maintenance and repairs.

• Finding Reliable Tenants: The Pillar of Property Management

Finding reliable tenants is akin to laying the cornerstone of your investment's success. Tenants who pay rent on time, respect the property, and adhere to lease terms form the bedrock of a prosperous rental venture. The process of securing such tenants involves a blend of marketing, communication, and thorough vetting.

Begin by creating compelling property listings that highlight the property's features and advantages. Clear photographs, detailed descriptions, and accurate information attract potential tenants and set the stage for successful tenant relationships.

Marketing isn't merely about casting a wide net; it's about targeting the right audience. Understand the demographics of your property's location and tailor your marketing efforts accordingly. This helps attract tenants who align with your property's attributes and your investment strategy.

Once inquiries start pouring in, effective communication becomes paramount. Promptly respond to queries, schedule property viewings, and make potential tenants feel valued. This positive experience at the outset lays the foundation for a harmonious tenant-landlord relationship.

- ## Leases, Tenant Screening, and Background Checks: Building Trust through Agreements

Crafting a solid lease agreement is more than a legal formality; it's a trust-building exercise that outlines the rights and responsibilities of both parties. An airtight lease not only safeguards your investment but also sets clear expectations for your tenants.

A well-drafted lease agreement covers critical aspects such as rent, security deposits, lease duration, maintenance responsibilities, and terms for termination. It establishes a framework that minimizes potential disputes and provides legal recourse in case of violations.

Tenant screening and background checks are essential components of successful property management. This process involves assessing potential tenants' financial stability, rental history, and criminal background. By conducting comprehensive screenings, you minimize the risk of leasing to tenants who might default on rent or engage in destructive behavior.

Screening criteria might include minimum income requirements, good rental history, and a clean criminal record. Employing a consistent screening process ensures fairness and legal compliance. While finding the right tenants might take longer, the benefits in terms of property preservation and hassle-free management are invaluable.

- ## Handling Maintenance and Repairs: Nurturing the Investment

Maintenance and repairs are the lifeblood of rental property management. A well-maintained property not only retains its value but also attracts quality tenants. Timely repairs and proactive maintenance contribute to tenant satisfaction, positive reviews, and long-term profitability.

Implement a maintenance plan that includes routine inspections and preventive measures. Regular inspections allow you to identify potential issues before they escalate, ensuring that minor repairs don't snowball into costly problems.

Respond promptly to tenant maintenance requests. Effective communication and swift action demonstrate your commitment to providing a comfortable living environment. Tenants who feel valued are more likely to renew leases, reducing turnover and vacancy costs.

For major repairs, prioritize transparency and communication. Inform tenants about the nature of the issue, the timeline for repairs, and any inconveniences they might experience. A well-informed tenant is more likely to be understanding and cooperative during the repair process.

In Conclusion: Orchestrating Excellence in Property Management.

Managing rental properties is an orchestration of skills, systems, and empathy. By finding reliable tenants who align with your property's vision, crafting effective leases and conducting thorough screenings, and adeptly handling maintenance and repairs, you're not just managing properties; you're orchestrating a symphony of tenant satisfaction, property preservation, and financial success. Each element, from the choice of tenants to the execution of repairs, contributes to the harmony of your investment journey. As you fine-tune your property management practices, you're not just nurturing properties; you're nurturing a legacy of excellence in real estate investment.

CHAPTER SEVEN

Maximizing Cash Flow and Returns: Sculpting Profits with Strategic Foresight

The pinnacle of real estate investment lies in the realm of maximizing cash flow and returns. It's the crescendo of financial success, where each decision and strategy harmoniously contribute to enhanced profitability. In this chapter, we embark on a journey to unlock the art of maximizing cash flow and returns. We'll explore strategies for increasing rental income, the essence of cost-effective property management, and the intricacies of tax planning for rental income.

- ### Strategies for Increasing Rental Income: Elevating Earnings

The pursuit of maximizing cash flow begins with the art of increasing rental income. This isn't just about adjusting numbers; it's about optimizing value, creating win-win scenarios for both landlords and tenants. By employing strategic tactics, you can elevate your rental income while delivering enhanced value to your tenants.

Consider implementing a rent review strategy. Regularly assessing the market and adjusting rental rates in alignment with prevailing conditions ensures that you're charging competitive rates. Incremental increases, particularly for long-term tenants, can boost revenue without causing undue financial strain.

Enhance your property's appeal through strategic upgrades. Adding desirable features such as energy-efficient appliances, modern finishes, or smart home technology can justify premium rental rates. Tenants are often willing to pay more for properties that offer convenience and a higher quality of living.

Exploring alternative income streams can also boost your bottom line. Consider services such as offering furnished rentals, providing on-site laundry facilities, or partnering with local businesses for exclusive tenant discounts. These value-add offerings can justify higher rents and improve tenant satisfaction.

- ## Cost-Effective Property Management: Balancing Quality and Efficiency

The heart of maximizing returns lies in cost-effective property management. Striking a delicate balance between maintaining quality standards and optimizing expenses is the key to preserving your cash flow. By adopting prudent practices, you can minimize costs while providing an exceptional living experience for tenants.

Regular maintenance and proactive repairs are the linchpin of cost-effective property management. Addressing minor issues promptly prevents them from snowballing into major repairs that drain your resources. A well-maintained property minimizes turnover costs and fosters tenant loyalty.

Efficiency extends beyond repairs to encompass operational practices. Utilize technology for streamlined communication, tenant applications, and rent collection. Online platforms can enhance efficiency while reducing administrative overhead.

Engaging professional property management services can be a strategic move. While it incurs a cost, the expertise, systems, and relationships these services offer can optimize property operations and potentially lead to higher rental income.

- ## Tax Planning for Rental Income: Unveiling Opportunities

The realm of tax planning is a treasure trove for real estate investors seeking to maximize cash flow. By navigating the intricacies of tax regulations and leveraging strategic approaches, you can unlock opportunities to reduce your tax liabilities and enhance your returns.

Understanding deductible expenses is crucial. Expenses related to property management, repairs, maintenance, mortgage interest, and property taxes are often deductible. By meticulously tracking these expenses, you can lower your taxable income and preserve more of your rental income.

Depreciation is a powerful tool that allows you to deduct a portion of the property's value over time. This deduction can offset rental income and reduce your tax liability. It's essential to consult with a tax professional to ensure accurate and compliant depreciation calculations.

1031 exchanges offer a mechanism to defer capital gains taxes by reinvesting proceeds from a property sale into another property. This strategy can potentially allow you to preserve more of your gains for reinvestment, contributing to overall portfolio growth.

In Conclusion: The Symphony of Financial Excellence

Maximizing cash flow and returns is the crescendo of your investment journey. By employing strategies for increasing rental income, adopting cost-effective property management practices, and embracing prudent tax planning, you're orchestrating a symphony of financial excellence. Each strategic decision and thoughtful approach harmoniously contribute to the melody of increased profitability and enduring success. As you continue to refine your strategies, you're not just maximizing returns; you're crafting a legacy of financial empowerment through real estate investment.

CHAPTER EIGHT

Scaling Your Real Estate Portfolio: Building Your Empire of Success

The journey of real estate investment is not merely a solitary pursuit; it's a symphony of growth, expansion, and evolution. As you embark on the path of scaling your real estate portfolio, you're not just accumulating properties; you're crafting an empire of success. In this chapter, we delve into the art of scaling your real estate portfolio, exploring the strategic maneuvers of refinancing and leveraging equity, the intricacies of expanding to multiple properties, and the transformational power of creating systems for efficiency.

- Refinancing and Leveraging Equity: Unveiling Hidden Potential

Refinancing isn't just a financial transaction; it's a gateway to unlocking hidden potential within your existing investments. By leveraging the equity you've amassed, you can fuel further acquisitions, enhance cash flow, and amplify your overall portfolio performance.

When refinancing, you essentially replace your existing mortgage with a new one, often at more favorable terms. This might lead to reduced interest rates, lower monthly payments, or extended loan terms. The freed-up cash flow can then be directed toward acquiring additional properties or improving existing ones.

Leveraging equity involves using the value of one property to secure financing for another. This strategy allows you to amplify your purchasing power, potentially acquiring multiple properties simultaneously. The increased scale of your portfolio translates to amplified rental income and enhanced long-term wealth-building prospects.

However, leveraging equity requires careful consideration. Assess your risk tolerance and financial capacity before embarking on this strategy. While leveraging can amplify gains, it also exposes you to increased liabilities. Crafting a well-balanced approach that aligns with your investment goals and risk profile is paramount.

- ## Expanding to Multiple Properties: The Symphony of Growth

Expanding your real estate portfolio to encompass multiple properties is the crescendo of scaling your investment empire. It's not merely a numerical increase; it's a symphony of strategic planning, diversification, and wealth accumulation. As you navigate this phase, consider these key strategies for effective expansion.

Diversification minimizes risk by spreading your investments across different properties and markets. Different types of properties, locations, and rental markets can offer stability and resilience against market fluctuations.

Systematic research is pivotal. Analyze potential properties meticulously, considering factors such as market trends, property conditions, and projected cash flows. Each acquisition should align with your overarching investment strategy and contribute to your portfolio's growth trajectory.

Financing remains a cornerstone. As you expand, consider how financing terms impact your portfolio's overall performance. Balance between short-term gains and long-term sustainability, and explore financing options that align with your expansion goals.

- ## Creating Systems for Efficiency: The Engine of Expansion

Scaling a real estate portfolio isn't just about acquiring more properties; it's about orchestrating efficiency that supports growth. The creation of systems, processes, and structures lays the foundation for seamless expansion, enabling you to manage and optimize your portfolio effectively.

Property management systems streamline tenant communication, rent collection, maintenance requests, and administrative tasks. These systems enhance tenant satisfaction and reduce operational inefficiencies.

Financial systems provide visibility into your portfolio's performance. Robust accounting and reporting practices enable you to track income, expenses, and profitability across multiple properties. This information guides strategic decisions and enhances overall financial management.

Professional partnerships can be transformative. Engaging property management companies, legal advisors, accountants, and real estate agents can provide expertise and support as you navigate the challenges of portfolio expansion.

In Conclusion: Building a Legacy of Success

Scaling your real estate portfolio isn't just about numbers; it's about crafting a legacy of success. By strategically refinancing and leveraging equity, expanding to multiple properties with diversification in mind, and creating efficient systems, you're not just scaling your investments; you're building a foundation for enduring prosperity. Each property acquired, each system implemented, contributes to the crescendo of your investment journey. As you continue to grow and expand, you're not just building a portfolio; you're sculpting an empire of success that stands as a testament to your vision, strategy, and dedication to real estate excellence.

CHAPTER NINE

Handling Challenges and Risks: Navigating the Realities of Investment

In the realm of real estate investment, challenges and risks are the companion shadows to potential rewards. As you journey through the intricate landscape of property ownership, it's not a question of whether challenges will arise; it's a matter of how well you navigate them. In this chapter, we delve into the art of handling challenges and risks, exploring the strategies for dealing with vacancies and turnovers, mitigating legal and liability issues, and adeptly adapting to market fluctuations.

- Dealing with Vacancies and Turnovers: The Ebb and Flow of Investment

Vacancies and turnovers are inherent parts of the rental property landscape. Just as tides ebb and flow, so do tenants in rental properties. While vacancies represent periods of uncertainty, turnovers offer the potential for renewal and growth. Navigating these phases with skill can mitigate the impact on your cash flow and property performance.

When a property becomes vacant, swift action is crucial. Begin by assessing the property's condition and making any necessary repairs or improvements. A well-maintained property enhances its appeal to potential tenants and minimizes the time it remains unoccupied.

Implement a proactive marketing strategy to attract new tenants swiftly. Leverage online platforms, social media, and professional photography to showcase the property's features. Accurate and compelling listings can expedite the process of finding suitable tenants.

Consider incentivizing lease renewals to reduce turnovers. Offer competitive rental rates, address tenant concerns promptly, and foster positive tenant-landlord relationships. A satisfied tenant is more likely to renew their lease, contributing to stable cash flow and reduced vacancy rates.

- ### Mitigating Legal and Liability Issues: Safeguarding Your Investment

The complex legal landscape surrounding real estate investment necessitates a vigilant approach to mitigate potential legal and liability issues. From rental agreements to property maintenance, a proactive stance can protect your investment and shield you from financial setbacks.

Craft a comprehensive and legally sound rental agreement. Clearly outline the terms, conditions, and responsibilities of both parties. Consult with legal experts to ensure that your agreement aligns with local laws and regulations.

Conduct thorough tenant screenings and background checks. This practice reduces the risk of leasing to tenants with a history of non-payment or property damage. By selecting tenants with strong rental histories, you minimize the potential for disputes and legal conflicts.

Prioritize property maintenance and repairs. Neglecting maintenance not only impacts tenant satisfaction but also exposes you to liability. Timely repairs ensure that the property remains safe and habitable, minimizing the risk of accidents or injuries.

- ### Adapting to Market Fluctuations: Thriving Amidst Change

The real estate market is characterized by its cyclical nature, with periods of stability followed by fluctuations. Adapting to market changes is not only essential; it's a hallmark of successful real estate investors. By adopting a flexible approach, you can navigate the shifting tides and emerge stronger in the face of uncertainty.

Stay informed about market trends and economic indicators. Understand the factors that influence property values, rental demand, and interest rates. This knowledge enables you to anticipate shifts and adjust your strategies accordingly.

Diversify your portfolio to enhance resilience. Owning properties in different locations and markets can help mitigate the impact of localized downturns. Diversity provides a safety net against market-specific fluctuations.

Maintain financial prudence by incorporating contingencies into your financial planning. Set aside reserves for unexpected vacancies, repairs, or market downturns. These reserves act as a buffer, allowing you to weather challenges without compromising your financial stability.

In Conclusion: The Art of Resilience

Handling challenges and risks in real estate investment is an art that requires resilience, strategic foresight, and adaptability. By effectively dealing with vacancies and turnovers, mitigating legal and liability issues, and adeptly adapting to market fluctuations, you're not just managing risks; you're mastering the art of navigating a complex landscape. Each challenge you overcome, each legal issue you mitigate, and each market fluctuation you adapt to contributes to your growth and evolution as an investor. As you continue to refine your strategies and navigate the ever-changing terrain of real estate, you're not just managing risks; you're sculpting a legacy of resilience and success.

CHAPTER TEN

Exit Strategies and Long-Term Wealth: Crafting Your Legacy of Prosperity

The culmination of a successful real estate investment journey lies not just in the present achievements but in the legacy you craft for the future. As you navigate the final phases of your journey, exit strategies and long-term wealth creation take center stage. This chapter delves into the art of planning exit strategies, exploring the considerations of selling vs. holding properties, the transformative power of 1031 exchanges and tax implications, and the visionary pursuit of building generational wealth.

- Selling vs. Holding Properties: Pivotal Decisions in Transition

The decision to sell or hold properties is a pivotal crossroads in the journey of real estate investment. Each choice carries distinct implications that resonate with your financial goals, market conditions, and long-term aspirations. Navigating this decision involves a blend of strategic foresight and introspection.

Selling properties offers liquidity and potential capital gains. When market conditions are favorable or when you've maximized returns on a property, selling can provide a substantial infusion of funds. This capital can be reinvested in other properties or diversified across different asset classes.

Holding properties, on the other hand, offers the potential for sustained cash flow and long-term appreciation. Properties that consistently generate positive cash flow can contribute to your financial stability, enabling you to weather economic fluctuations. Holding properties can also lead to generational wealth, with properties passed down to heirs over time.

- 1031 Exchanges and Tax Implications: The Power of Continuity

The 1031 exchange is a strategic tool that empowers real estate investors to defer capital gains taxes by reinvesting proceeds from a property sale into a replacement property. This exchange allows you to maintain the continuity of your investments, potentially amplifying your portfolio growth.

A successful 1031 exchange requires adherence to strict guidelines and timelines. The proceeds from the initial property's sale must be used to acquire a replacement property of equal or greater value within a specific timeframe. Consulting with a tax professional and a qualified intermediary is crucial to ensure compliance with the intricate regulations.

Tax implications play a significant role in exit strategies. While selling properties can trigger capital gains taxes, exchanging properties through a 1031 exchange can offer tax deferral benefits. Understanding the tax consequences of your decisions is essential to align your exit strategy with your financial objectives.

- Building Generational Wealth: The Visionary Pursuit

As you approach the final stages of your real estate investment journey, the concept of building generational wealth comes to the forefront. This visionary pursuit transcends immediate gains, focusing on the legacy you leave for future generations.

Generational wealth is built by strategically passing down properties and assets to heirs. Proper estate planning ensures a smooth transition of assets, minimizing tax implications and legal complications. Engage with legal and financial experts to craft a comprehensive estate plan that aligns with your vision.

The pursuit of generational wealth isn't just about tangible assets; it's also about instilling financial literacy and values in future generations. Educate your heirs about the principles of responsible wealth management, enabling them to continue building on the foundation you've laid.

In Conclusion: Crafting a Legacy of Prosperity

Exit strategies and long-term wealth creation mark the culmination of your real estate investment journey. By carefully considering the choice between selling and holding properties, leveraging the power of 1031 exchanges and understanding tax implications, and envisioning the pursuit of generational wealth, you're not just wrapping up investments; you're crafting a legacy of prosperity.

Each property you decide to sell or hold, each exchange you execute, and each generational wealth plan you put in place contributes to the symphony of your investment journey. As you transition from an active investor to a visionary architect of your legacy, you're not just building wealth; you're sculpting a legacy that echoes through generations, embodying the values, wisdom, and foresight you've cultivated on this remarkable journey.

CHAPTER ELEVEN

Case Studies and Success Stories: Illuminating the Path of Achievement

The journey of real estate investment is rich with stories of triumph, strategies that worked, and lessons learned from the trenches. In this chapter, we delve into the world of case studies and success stories, exploring real-life examples of successful investments and the invaluable lessons gleaned from experienced investors. These narratives serve as beacons of inspiration, offering insights into the art and science of real estate achievement.

- ### Real-Life Examples of Successful Investments: The Tapestry of Triumph

Case studies of successful investments are like threads woven into the tapestry of real estate achievement. Each story presents a unique scenario, strategy, and outcome, offering a diverse array of insights for aspiring and seasoned investors alike. Let's explore a few illustrative case studies that exemplify the spectrum of possibilities within real estate investment.

Case Study 1: The Renovation Revolution

An investor acquires a rundown property in an up-and-coming neighborhood. Through careful planning, strategic renovations, and tenant-centered improvements, the property's value skyrockets. The investor capitalizes on the surge in demand, ultimately selling the property for a substantial profit. Key takeaways include the power of targeted renovations, the impact of location on value appreciation, and the importance of understanding local market trends.

Case Study 2: The Cash Flow Conquest

In a market with consistent demand for rental properties, an investor assembles a portfolio of cash-flow-positive units. By focusing on properties that generate steady income and employing effective property management practices, the investor enjoys consistent monthly cash flow and long-term stability. This case underscores the significance of thorough due diligence, effective property management, and aligning investments with local rental demand.

- Lessons Learned from Experienced Investors: The Wisdom of the Trailblazers

Learning from experienced investors is akin to receiving a treasure trove of wisdom. The lessons they've learned from successes and setbacks are invaluable guideposts for those who seek to follow in their footsteps. Let's delve into some key lessons shared by seasoned investors.

Lesson 1: Due Diligence is Non-Negotiable

Experienced investors emphasize the importance of meticulous due diligence. Research the property, market trends, and tenant demographics. This not only helps you make informed decisions but also minimizes the risk of surprises down the road.

Lesson 2: Adaptability is a Virtue

The real estate landscape is dynamic. Market conditions change, tenant preferences evolve, and economic trends fluctuate. Successful investors stress the importance of adaptability. Be willing to pivot your strategy, adjust your approach, and remain open to new opportunities.

Lesson 3: Relationships Matter

Building and nurturing relationships within the real estate ecosystem can be a catalyst for success. Networking with other investors, real estate professionals, and mentors provides access to valuable insights, resources, and potential partnerships.

In Conclusion: Illuminating the Path Forward

Case studies and success stories serve as guiding lights on the path of real estate investment. Through real-life examples of successful investments and the lessons shared by experienced investors, you gain a multifaceted perspective on the strategies, pitfalls, and triumphs that define the journey.

As you absorb these narratives, remember that each story contributes to your own knowledge, growth, and strategy development. By applying the lessons learned and drawing inspiration from the successes of others, you're not just navigating your investment journey; you're shaping your own unique narrative of real estate achievement.

CHAPTER TWELVE

Insights from experienced investors:

Insights from experienced investors are like pearls of wisdom gleaned from years of hands-on experience in the real estate arena. Here are some valuable insights that these seasoned individuals often share:

Start with Education: Before diving into investments, educate yourself thoroughly about the real estate market, local regulations, financing options, and investment strategies. Knowledge is the foundation upon which successful decisions are made.

Location is Paramount: The age-old adage "location, location, location" holds true. Investing in properties situated in desirable neighborhoods with potential for growth is a key factor in long-term success.

Long-Term Vision: Real estate investment is not a get-rich-quick scheme. Adopt a long-term perspective, focusing on building wealth steadily over time. Patient investors often see the best returns.

Cash Flow is King: Positive cash flow is the lifeblood of your investments. Prioritize properties that generate consistent rental income after covering all expenses. Sustainable cash flow safeguards against market downturns.

Diversification Mitigates Risk: Spreading your investments across different property types and markets reduces risk. A diversified portfolio is better equipped to withstand market fluctuations.

Know Your Numbers: Thoroughly analyze each property's potential returns and risks. This includes calculating expenses, projected rental income, potential appreciation, and understanding financing terms.

Network and Learn: Building relationships within the real estate community is invaluable. Networking with other investors, attending seminars, and seeking advice from mentors can accelerate your learning curve.

Adapt to Market Trends: Real estate markets change over time. Savvy investors adapt their strategies to align with evolving market trends, whether it's focusing on short-term rentals, sustainable properties, or emerging neighborhoods.

Leverage Professionals: Engaging experts like real estate agents, property managers, legal advisors, and accountants can provide specialized knowledge and support critical decision-making.

Be Mindful of Debt: While leveraging can amplify gains, overleveraging can lead to financial strain. Maintain a healthy balance between debt and equity to weather economic uncertainties.

Embrace Creativity: Creative solutions can yield impressive results. Look for distressed properties with potential, consider alternative financing options, and explore unconventional investment strategies.

Plan for Contingencies: Real estate isn't immune to unexpected challenges. Set aside reserves for vacancies, repairs, and market downturns to ensure your investment remains resilient.

Keep Emotions in Check: Investment decisions should be based on facts and analysis, not emotions. Avoid getting attached to properties and focus on their financial potential.

Continuous Learning: Real estate is an evolving field. Commit to continuous learning to stay updated on industry trends, new regulations, and innovative investment strategies.

Stay Disciplined: Stick to your investment plan and resist the temptation to deviate based on short-term market fluctuations. Consistency is a hallmark of successful investors.

These insights serve as guiding principles that have helped experienced investors navigate the intricate terrain of real estate investment. Learning from their experiences can provide you with a solid foundation as you embark on your own journey to real estate success.

Conclusion:

Embracing the Journey Ahead

As you reach the conclusion of this comprehensive exploration into the world of real estate investment, you stand at the threshold of a remarkable journey. Your understanding of the art and science of real estate has expanded, and you're equipped with a toolkit of knowledge, strategies, and insights to embark on your own path of investment success.

The journey of real estate investment is one of continual growth, learning, and evolution. It's a journey that demands a blend of strategic foresight, adaptability, and unwavering determination. As you step forward, remember that each decision you make, each property you acquire, and each challenge you overcome contributes to the symphony of your investment story.

- ## The Journey Ahead: Building Your Legacy

Your journey in real estate investment is not a linear path; it's a mosaic of opportunities, challenges, triumphs, and growth. Whether you're just beginning or have already started, your journey unfolds with each property you acquire, each strategy you employ, and each lesson you learn.

Consider this journey as the sculpting of your legacy—a legacy of financial empowerment, strategic acumen, and visionary thinking. Each property becomes a brushstroke, each challenge an opportunity to refine your skills, and each success a testament to your commitment to excellence.

- ## Continuing Your Education in Real Estate: An Ever-Evolving Path

The world of real estate is in a constant state of flux, with market dynamics, regulations, and trends continuously evolving. Your education doesn't conclude here; it's an ongoing pursuit. As you navigate the landscape of real estate investment, commit to staying informed, learning from experiences, and embracing new knowledge.

Continuing education might involve attending workshops, reading industry publications, joining real estate investment clubs, and networking with fellow investors. As you deepen your expertise, you'll find yourself better equipped to navigate challenges, seize opportunities, and make informed decisions.

In Conclusion: Your Legacy Awaits

The journey of real estate investment is an exciting, transformative, and rewarding endeavor. It's a journey that has the potential to shape your financial future, empower your dreams, and leave a lasting legacy for generations to come.

As you take the next steps, remember that every success, every challenge, and every strategy you employ is a testament to your dedication to this remarkable journey. With your newfound knowledge and unwavering determination, you're sculpting a legacy that transcends bricks and mortar—it's a legacy of achievement, empowerment, and prosperity. Your journey awaits, and your legacy begins now.